14 designs by Marie Wallin
using Rowan Purelife
British Sheep Breeds Chunky, DK, Bouclé &
Purelife Renew

purelife home

Knitted accessories for the home have recently seen a resurgence of interest with fashionable interior magazines promoting traditional hand knitted cushions and throws as well as more unusual art pieces, rugs and furniture coverings. There has been a growing confidence in knit design for interiors over the past few seasons, which not only pushes the boundaries of textile use in interiors but importantly commemorates the longstanding craft of hand knitting and crochet.

Purelife Home is a reaction to this important trend. The collection showcases wonderful rugs, throws and cushions as well as table mats and pouffe cushions. By using our lovely British Sheep Breeds and Renew yarns you can be assured that not only will you be creating amazing unique pieces for the fashion conscious home but you will also be helping the British hill farmer, British yarn manufacture and the environment.

Marie Wallin

textured rug
british sheep breeds chunky & bouclé
pattern page 48

tweed throw
renew
pattern page 49

felted placemat
british sheep breeds chunky & DK
pattern page 39

19 06
RONALD RVTHVEN
EARL OF LEVEN AND MELVILLE

granny squares throw
renew
pattern page 42

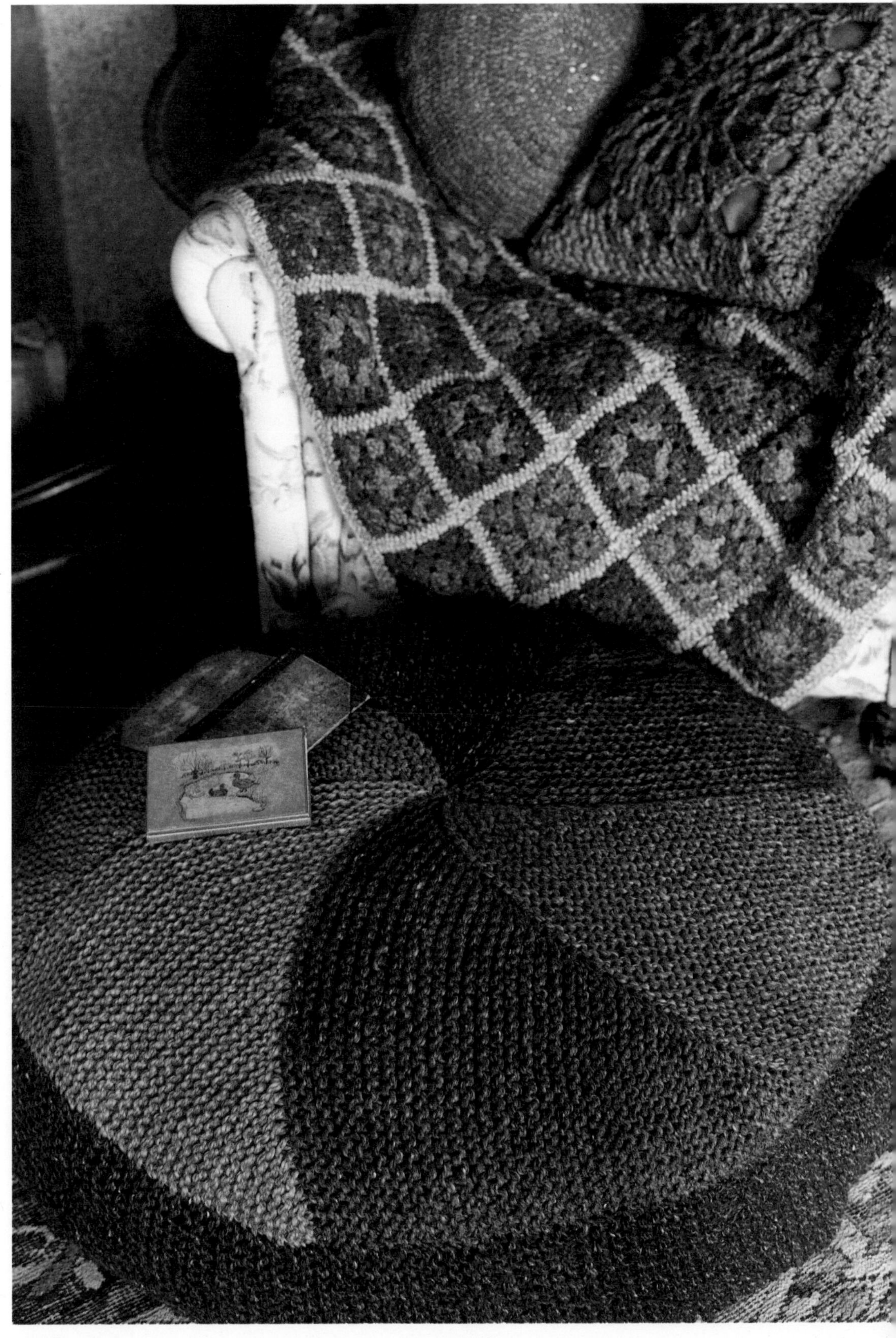

garter stitch pouffe
renew
pattern page 40

garter stitch throw
british sheep breeds chunky & bouclé
pattern page 41

tweed, crochet granny squares & crochet squares throws
all in renew
pattern page 49 (tweed), 42 (granny squares)
38 (crochet squares)

RT HON
THE EARL OF
LEVEN & MELVILLE
No 3
GLENFERNESS

mini graphic, two tone stripe,
plain & striped crochet circular cushions
all in british sheep breeds DK
pattern page 46(mini graphic), 51 (two tone stripe)
36 (plain & striped crochet circle)

crochet doily rug
british sheep breeds bouclé
pattern page 35

plain & striped crochet circular & lattice spot cushions
british sheep breeds chunky, bouclé & DK
pattern page 36 (plain & striped crochet circle) 45 (lattice spot)

plaited placemat
renew
pattern page 47

crochet square & crochet stripe circular cushions on granny squares throw
all in renew
pattern page 43 (crochet squares) 37 (crochet stripe) 42 (granny squares throw)

A PASSION
GROUSE
SCOTTISH
WILD
FLOWERS
Mary McMurtrie

crochet square, crochet plain & stripe circular cushions
all in renew

crochet squares throw & graphic squares cushion
all in renew
pattern page 38 (crochet squares throw) 44 (graphic squares)

Purelife British Sheep Breeds Yarns

As we start to demand transparency on how and where our food, fashion and white goods come from, we are seeing the popularity of home produced yarns increase. Our British Sheep Breeds range of yarns have an authenticity that is inherent within the yarns themselves – hundreds of years of character and culture spun into beautiful rugged yarns that have an integrity that you don't seem to get from yarns made in the modern mills of Italy and the rest of Europe. They may be more expensive but that is because they are made from British native breeds and spun in our very own Yorkshire – British hill farmers and domestic manufacturing definitely worth preserving for future generations.

THE BREEDS

Black Welsh

In Wales this sheep is known as 'Cochddu' meaning 'brownish'. This hardy sheep produces fleece which is black, short and thick with a firm handle, durable, light weight and warm.

Shetland Moorit

The Shetland breed of sheep is a small, hardy animal producing fine soft wool.
They are farmed on the Shetland Islands but are now more commonly found throughout the UK. Their wool is used exclusively for knitwear, fine shawls and soft woven fabrics.

Jacob

Jacob sheep are generally considered to be an ornamental breed and are often adorned with two, four or even six horns. They are believed to originate from Mesopotamia in Biblical times. The fleece produces naturally blended shades of brown and creamy white.

Suffolk

These sheep are widely spread throughout the United Kingdom. The fleece is moderately short with fine fibres.

Bluefaced Leicester

Wool of the Bluefaced Leicester is fairly fine, dense and demi-lustrous, soft to the touch, drapes well and feels comfortable next to the skin.

Masham

Masham is a hardy breed with a good reputation for quality lambs. The Masham ewe is medium sized and hornless and produces fleece in long staples, 8-10 inches on a yearling and 6 to 7 inches on a ewe, with a good degree of lustre.

HE YARNS

ritish Sheep Breeds Chunky

bluefaced leicester
950

black welsh
951

mid brown jacob
952

dark grey welsh
953

steel grey suffolk
954

shetland moorit
955

light masham
957

British Sheep Breeds DK

bluefaced leicester
780

brown bluefaced leicester
781

mid brown bluefaced leicester
782

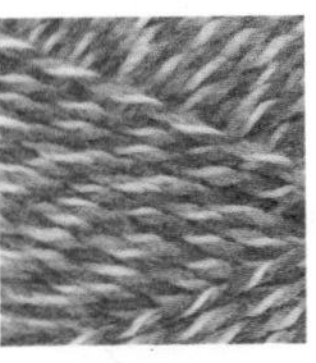
bluefaced leicester marl
783

bluefaced leicester grey suffolk
784

bluefaced leicester mid brown jacob
785

British Sheep Breeds Bouclé

ecru
220

light brown masham
221

mid brown masham
222

dark brown masham
223

Purelife Renew

Made from recycled wool this wonderful yarn is available in the 10 vibrant and tweedy shades shown below. Since the launch o Renew in 2010, it is fast becoming a popular yarn. The rustic nature and character of the yarn make it the perfect choice for makin home interior pieces which will wear and perform well.

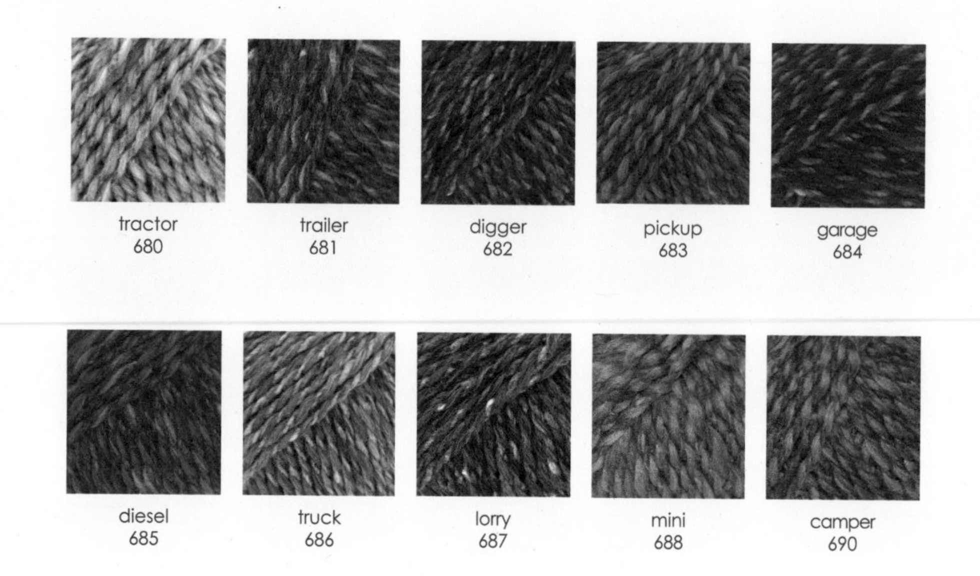

crochet doily rug

main image page 19

YARN
Rowan Purelife British Sheep Breeds Boucle
7 x 100gm
(photographed in Ecru 220)

CROCHET HOOK
15mm (US P19) crochet hook

TENSION
First 2 rounds measure 22 cm in diameter using 15mm (US P19) crochet hook and yarn DOUBLE.

FINISHED SIZE
Completed mat measures approx 105 cm (41½ ins) in diameter.

CROCHET ABBREVIATIONS

ch = chain; **dc** = double crochet; **dtr** = double treble; **dtr3tog** = *(yoh) twice and insert hook as indicated, yoh and draw loop through, (yoh and draw through 2 loops) twice, rep from * twice more, yoh and draw through all 4 loops on hook; **dtr4tog** = *(yoh) twice and insert hook as indicated, yoh and draw loop through, (yoh and draw through 2 loops) twice, rep from * 3 times more, yoh and draw through all 5 loops on hook; **htr** = half treble; **sp(s)** = space(s); **ss** = slip stitch; **tr** = treble; **ttr** = triple treble; **ttr3tog** = *(yoh) 3 times and insert hook as indicated, yoh and draw loop through, (yoh and draw through 2 loops) 3 times, rep from * twice more, yoh and draw through all 4 loops on hook; **ttr4tog** = *(yoh) 3 times and insert hook as indicated, yoh and draw loop through, (yoh and draw through 2 loops) 3 times, rep from * 3 times more, yoh and draw through all 5 loops on hook; **yoh** = yarn over hook.

RUG

Using 15mm (US P19) hook and yarn DOUBLE make 6 ch and join with a ss to form a ring.
Round 1 (RS): 5 ch (counts as 1 tr and 2 ch), (1 tr into ring, 2 ch) 7 times, ss to 3rd of 5 ch at beg of round.
Round 2: 3 ch (counts as 1 tr), miss st at base of 3 ch, (4 tr into next ch sp, 1 tr into next tr) 7 times, 4 tr into last ch sp, ss to top of 3 ch at beg of round. 40 sts.
Round 3: Ss into next tr, 3 ch (counts as 1 tr), miss st at base of 3 ch, *1 dc into each of next 2 tr, 1 tr into next tr, 5 ch, miss 1 tr**, 1 tr into next tr, rep from * to end, ending last rep at **, ss to top of 3 ch at beg of round.
Round 4: 4 ch (does NOT count as st), dtr3tog over next 3 sts, *6 ch, 1 dc into next ch sp, 6 ch**, dtr4tog over next 4 sts, rep from * to end, ending last rep at **, ss to top of dtr3tog at beg of round.
Round 5: 11 ch (counts as 1 ttr and 6 ch), *1 dc into next ch sp, 1 dc into next dc, 1 dc into next ch sp, 6 ch**, 1 ttr into next dtr4tog, 6 ch, rep from * to end, ending last rep at **, ss to 5th of 11 ch at beg of round.
Round 6: 13 ch (counts as 1 ttr and 8 ch), *miss (next ch sp and 1 dc), 1 dc into next dc**, 8 ch, miss (1 dc and next ch sp), 1 ttr into next ttr, 8 ch, rep from * to end, ending last rep at **, 6 ch, 1 htr to 5th of 13 ch at beg of round.
Round 7: 3 ch (counts as 1 tr), 1 tr into ch sp partly formed by htr at end of previous round, *miss 1 ttr, 2 tr into next ch sp, 12 ch, miss next dc**, 2 tr into next ch sp, rep from * to end, ending last rep at **, ss to top of 3 ch at beg of round.
Round 8: 5 ch (does NOT count as st), miss st at base of 5 ch, ttr3tog over next 3 sts, *10 ch, ttr4tog into next ch sp, 10 ch**, ttr4tog over next 4 tr, rep from * to end, ending last rep at **, ss to top of ttr3tog at beg of round.
Round 9: 7 ch (counts as 1 tr and 4 ch), 1 tr into st at base of 7 ch, *(4 ch and 1 tr) 5 times into next ch sp, 4 ch**, (1 tr, 4 ch and 1 tr) into next ttr4tog, rep from * to end, ending last rep at **, ss to 3rd of 7 ch at beg of round.
Fasten off.

MAKING UP

Press as described on the information page.
If desired, mat can be framed and hung on the wall. To do this, cut a square of firm backing board at least 110 cm square. Apply spray adhesive to WS of mat and then apply mat to backing board. Frame mat inside a deep box frame.

plain & striped crochet circular cushions

main image page 19 & 20

YARN
Rowan Purelife British Sheep Breeds DK
Plain cushion
4 x 50gm
(photographed in Bluefaced Leicester 780)
Striped cushion
A Brown Bluefaced Leicester
781 1 x 50gm
B Mid Brown Bluefaced Leicester
782 2 x 50gm
C Bluefaced Leicester
780 1 x 50gm

CROCHET HOOK
4.00mm (no 8) (US G6) crochet hook

EXTRAS - 35 cm (14 in) diameter circular cushion pad

TENSION
First 4 rounds meas 10 cm in diameter using 4.00mm (US G6) crochet hook.

CROCHET ABBREVIATIONS
ch = chain; **ss** = slip stitch; **tr** = treble.

Plain cushion

Using same colour throughout, work as given for striped cushion (see below).

Striped cushion

CIRCLES (make 2)
Using 4.00mm (US G6) hook and yarn A make 5 ch and join with a ss to form a ring.
Joining in and breaking off colours as required, cont as folls:
Round 1 (RS): Using yarn A, 3 ch (counts as 1 tr), 12 tr into ring, ss to top of 3 ch at beg of round. 13 sts.
Round 2: Using yarn B, 3 ch (counts as 1 tr), 1 tr into st at base of 3 ch, 2 tr into each tr to end, ss to top of 3 ch at beg of round. 26 sts.
Round 3: Using yarn C, 3 ch (counts as 1 tr), miss st at base of 3 ch, 2 tr into next tr, (1 tr into next tr, 2 tr into next tr) 12 times, ss to top of 3 ch at beg of round. 39 sts.
Round 4: Using yarn B, 3 ch (counts as 1 tr), miss st at base of 3 ch, 2 tr into next tr, (1 tr into each of next 2 tr, 2 tr into next tr) 12 times, 1 tr into next tr, ss to top of 3 ch at beg of round. 52 sts.
Round 5: Using yarn A, 3 ch (counts as 1 tr), miss st at base of 3 ch, 2 tr into next tr, (1 tr into each of next 3 tr, 2 tr into next tr) 12 times, 1 tr into each of next 2 tr, ss to top of 3 ch at beg of round. 65 sts.
Round 6: Using yarn B, 3 ch (counts as 1 tr), miss st at base of 3 ch, 2 tr into next tr, (1 tr into each of next 4 tr, 2 tr into next tr) 12 times, 1 tr into each of next 3 tr, ss to top of 3 ch at beg of round. 78 sts.
Round 7: Using yarn C, 3 ch (counts as 1 tr), miss st at base of 3 ch, 2 tr into next tr, (1 tr into each of next 5 tr, 2 tr into next tr) 12 times, 1 tr into each of next 4 tr, ss to top of 3 ch at beg of round. 91 sts.
Round 8: Using yarn B, 3 ch (counts as 1 tr), miss st at base of 3 ch, 2 tr into next tr, (1 tr into each of next 6 tr, 2 tr into next tr) 12 times, 1 tr into each of next 5 tr, ss to top of 3 ch at beg of round. 104 sts.
Round 9: Using yarn A, 3 ch (counts as 1 tr), miss st at base of 3 ch, 2 tr into next tr, (1 tr into each of next 7 tr, 2 tr into next tr) 12 times, 1 tr into each of next 6 tr, ss to top of 3 ch at beg of round. 117 sts.
Round 10: Using yarn B, 3 ch (counts as 1 tr), miss st at base of 3 ch, 2 tr into next tr, (1 tr into each of next 8 tr, 2 tr into next tr) 12 times, 1 tr into each of next 7 tr, ss to top of 3 ch at beg of round. 130 sts.
Round 11: Using yarn C, 3 ch (counts as 1 tr), miss st at base of 3 ch, 2 tr into next tr, (1 tr into each of next 9 tr, 2 tr into next tr) 12 times, 1 tr into each of next 8 tr, ss to top of 3 ch at beg of round. 143 sts.
Round 12: Using yarn B, 3 ch (counts as 1 tr), miss st at base of 3 ch, 2 tr into next tr, (1 tr into each of next 10 tr, 2 tr into next tr) 12 times, 1 tr into each of next 9 tr, ss to top of 3 ch at beg of round. 156 sts.
Round 13: Using yarn A, 3 ch (counts as 1 tr), miss st at base of 3 ch, 2 tr into next tr, (1 tr into each of next 11 tr, 2 tr into next tr) 12 times, 1 tr into each of next 10 tr, ss to top of 3 ch at beg of round. 169 sts.
Round 14: Using yarn B, 3 ch (counts as 1 tr), miss st at base of 3 ch, 2 tr into next tr, (1 tr into each of next 12 tr, 2 tr into next tr) 12 times, 1 tr into each of next 11 tr, ss to top of 3 ch at beg of round. 182 sts.
Round 15: Using yarn B, 3 ch (counts as 1 tr), miss st at base of 3 ch, 2 tr into next tr, (1 tr into each of next 13 tr, 2 tr into next tr) 12 times, 1 tr into each of next 12 tr, ss to top of 3 ch at beg of round. 195 sts.
Fasten off.

MAKING UP
Press as described on the information page.
Join circles around outer edges, inserting cushion pad before closing edges.

plain & striped crochet circular cushions

main image page 24

YARN
Rowan Purelife Renew
Striped cushion

A Trailer	681	1	x 50gm
B Pick Up	683	2	x 50gm
C Mini	688	1	x 50gm
D Tractor	680	1	x 50gm
E Camper	690	1	x 50gm
Plain cushion			
		5	x 50gm

(photographed in Pick Up 683)

CROCHET HOOK
6.00mm (no 4) (US J10) crochet hook

EXTRAS - 35 cm (14 in) diameter circular cushion pad for striped cushion, or 40 cm (16 in) diameter circular cushion pad for plain cushion

TENSION
First 3 rounds meas 11 cm in diameter using 6.00mm (US J10) crochet hook.

CROCHET ABBREVIATIONS
ch = chain; **ss** = slip stitch; **tr** = treble.

Striped cushion

CIRCLES (make 2)
Using 6.00mm (US J10) hook and yarn A make 5 ch and join with a ss to form a ring.
Joining in and breaking off colours as required, cont as folls:
Round 1 (RS): Using yarn A, 3 ch (counts as 1 tr), 15 tr into ring, ss to top of 3 ch at beg of round. 16 sts.
Round 2: Using yarn B, 3 ch (counts as 1 tr), 1 tr into st at base of 3 ch, 2 tr into each tr to end, ss to top of 3 ch at beg of round. 32 sts.
Round 3: Using yarn C, 3 ch (counts as 1 tr), miss st at base of 3 ch, 2 tr into next tr, (1 tr into next tr, 2 tr into next tr) 15 times, ss to top of 3 ch at beg of round. 48 sts.
Round 4: Using yarn D, 3 ch (counts as 1 tr), miss st at base of 3 ch, 2 tr into next tr, (1 tr into each of next 2 tr, 2 tr into next tr) 15 times, 1 tr into next tr, ss to top of 3 ch at beg of round. 64 sts.
Round 5: Using yarn E, 3 ch (counts as 1 tr), miss st at base of 3 ch, 2 tr into next tr, (1 tr into each of next 3 tr, 2 tr into next tr) 15 times, 1 tr into each of next 2 tr, ss to top of 3 ch at beg of round. 80 sts.
Round 6: Using yarn B, 3 ch (counts as 1 tr), miss st at base of 3 ch, 2 tr into next tr, (1 tr into each of next 4 tr, 2 tr into next tr) 15 times, 1 tr into each of next 3 tr, ss to top of 3 ch at beg of round. 96 sts.
Round 7: Using yarn A, 3 ch (counts as 1 tr), miss st at base of 3 ch, 2 tr into next tr, (1 tr into each of next 5 tr, 2 tr into next tr) 15 times, 1 tr into each of next 4 tr, ss to top of 3 ch at beg of round. 112 sts.
Round 8: Using yarn C, 3 ch (counts as 1 tr), miss st at base of 3 ch, 2 tr into next tr, (1 tr into each of next 6 tr, 2 tr into next tr) 15 times, 1 tr into each of next 5 tr, ss to top of 3 ch at beg of round. 128 sts.
Round 9: Using yarn E, 3 ch (counts as 1 tr), miss st at base of 3 ch, 2 tr into next tr, (1 tr into each of next 7 tr, 2 tr into next tr) 15 times, 1 tr into each of next 6 tr, ss to top of 3 ch at beg of round. 144 sts.
Round 10: Using yarn D, 3 ch (counts as 1 tr), miss st at base of 3 ch, 2 tr into next tr, (1 tr into each of next 8 tr, 2 tr into next tr) 15 times, 1 tr into each of next 7 tr, ss to top of 3 ch at beg of round. 160 sts.
Round 11: Using yarn B, 3 ch (counts as 1 tr), miss st at base of 3 ch, 2 tr into next tr, (1 tr into each of next 9 tr, 2 tr into next tr) 15 times, 1 tr into each of next 8 tr, ss to top of 3 ch at beg of round. 176 sts.
Fasten off.

MAKING UP
Press as described on the information page.
Join circles around outer edges, inserting cushion pad before closing edges.

Plain cushion

CIRCLES (make 2)
Using same colour throughout, work as given for circles of striped cushion to end of round 11.
Round 12: 3 ch (counts as 1 tr), miss st at base of 3 ch, 2 tr into next tr, (1 tr into each of next 10 tr, 2 tr into next tr) 15 times, 1 tr into each of next 9 tr, ss to top of 3 ch at beg of round. 192 sts.
Fasten off.

MAKING UP
Press as described on the information page.
Join circles around outer edges, inserting cushion pad before closing edges.

crochet squares throw

main image page 28

YARN

Rowan Purelife Renew

A Trailer	681	5	x 50gm
B Pick Up	683	5	x 50gm
C Garage	684	5	x 50gm
D Camper	690	5	x 50gm
E Mini	688	5	x 50gm
F Diesel	685	5	x 50gm
G Digger	682	7	x 50gm

CROCHET HOOK

15mm (US P19) crochet hook

TENSION

Basic motif meas 38 cm square using 15mm (US P19) crochet hook and yarn DOUBLE.

FINISHED SIZE

Completed throw measures 126 cm (49½ ins) by 167 cm (65½ ins).

CROCHET ABBREVIATIONS

ch = chain; **dc** = double crochet; **sp(s)** = space(s); **ss** = slip stitch; **tr** = treble.

MOTIFS (make 12)

Using 15mm (US P19) hook and yarn A DOUBLE make 6 ch and join with a ss to form a ring.

Round 1 (RS): 3 ch (counts as 1 tr), 15 tr into ring, ss to top of 3 ch at beg of round.

Round 2: 5 ch (counts as 1 tr and 2 ch), miss st at base of 5 ch, (1 tr into next tr, 2 ch) 15 times, ss to 3rd of 5 ch at beg of round.

Round 3: Ss into first ch sp, 3 ch (counts as 1 tr), 2 tr into ch sp at base of 3 ch, 1 ch, (3 tr into next ch sp, 1 ch) 15 times, ss to top of 3 ch at beg of round.

Round 4: Ss across and into first ch sp, 1 ch (does NOT count as st), 1 dc into ch sp at base of 1 ch, 3 ch, miss 3 tr, 1 dc into next ch sp, 6 ch, miss 3 tr, *1 dc into next ch sp, (3 ch, miss 3 tr, 1 dc into next ch sp) 3 times, 6 ch, miss 3 tr, rep from * twice more, (1 dc into next ch sp, 3 ch, miss 3 tr) twice, ss to first dc.

Round 5: Ss into first 3-ch sp, 3 ch (counts as 1 tr), 2 tr into ch sp at base of 3 ch, *(5 tr, 2 ch and 5 tr) into next 6-ch sp, (3 tr into next 3-ch sp) 3 times, rep from * twice more, (5 tr, 2 ch and 5 tr) into next 6-ch sp, (3 tr into next 3-ch sp) twice, ss to top of 3 ch at beg of round.

Round 6: 3 ch (counts as 1 tr), miss st at base of 3 ch, 1 tr into each of next 7 tr, *(3 tr, 2 ch and 3 tr) into next ch sp, 1 tr into each of next 19 tr, rep from * twice more, (3 tr, 2 ch and 3 tr) into next ch sp, 1 tr into each of next 11 tr, ss to top of 3 ch at beg of round.

Fasten off.

Completed motif is a square. In each corner there is a 2-ch sp and along each side, between the corner ch sps, there are 25 tr. 27 sts (25 tr and 2 ch) along each side of motif.

Remembering to use yarn DOUBLE throughout, now make a further 11 motifs in colours as folls: 1 more motif using yarn A, and 2 motifs in each of yarns B, C, D, E and F - 12 motifs in total.

THROW

Join motifs into strips

Following diagram, join motifs into strips as folls: With RS facing, 15mm (US P19) hook and yarn G DOUBLE, attach yarn to corner ch sp of first motif, 3 ch (counts as 1 tr), holding RS of next motif against RS of first motif, work 1 ss into correspond corner ch sp of 2nd motif, (1 tr into next tr of first motif, 1 ss into correspond tr of 2nd motif) 25 times, 1 tr into next corner ch sp of first motif, 1 ss into corresponding corner ch sp of 2nd motif.

Fasten off.

Following diagram, cont to join motifs to form 4 strips of 3 motifs.

Join strips

Following diagram, join strips into one large rectangle as folls:

With RS facing, 15mm (US P19) hook and yarn G DOUBLE, attach yarn to corner ch sp of end motif of first strip, 3 ch (counts as 1 tr), holding RS of end motif of next strip against RS of end motif of first strip, work 1 ss into correspond corner ch sp of 2nd strip motif, *(1 tr into next tr of first motif, 1 ss into correspond tr of 2nd motif) 25 times, 1 tr into next corner ch sp of first motif, 1 ss into corresponding corner ch sp of 2nd motif, now join strips across row joining motifs as folls: (1 tr around stem of tr joining first strip, 1 ss around corresponding tr joining 2nd strip) twice, cont in this way until all 3 motifs of strips are joined.

Fasten off.

Edging

With RS facing, 15mm (US P19) hook and yarn G DOUBLE, attach yarn along one side of joined motifs, 3 ch (counts as 1 tr), miss st at base of 3 ch, now work one round of tr around entire outer edge of joined motifs, working 1 tr into each tr and ch sp along edges of motifs, 2 tr around stem of tr joining motifs and strips, and 3 tr into ch sps at corners, and ending with ss to top of 3 ch at beg of round.

Fasten off.

Press as described on the information page.

F	E	D
A	C	B
E	D	F
C	B	A

felted place mat

main image page 10

YARN

Rowan Purelife British Sheep Breeds Chunky and DK

A Chunky Mid Brown Jacob

952 1 x 100gm

B DK Mid Brown Bluefaced Leicester

782 1 x 50gm

NEEDLES

1 pair 7mm (no 2) (US 10 1/2) needles

3.00mm (no 11) (US C2) crochet hook

TENSION

Before felting, 13 sts and 18 rows to 10 cm measured over st st using 7mm (US 10 1/2) needles and yarn A.

FINISHED SIZE

Completed mat measures 38 cm (15 ins) in diameter.

CROCHET ABBREVIATIONS

ch = chain; **dc** = double crochet; **sp(s)** = space(s); **ss** = slip stitch; **tr** = treble.

CENTRE SECTION

Using 7mm (US 10½) needles and yarn A cast on 44 sts.

Beg with a K row, work in st st for 31 cm, ending with RS facing for next row.

Cast off.

Hot machine wash and tumble dry centre section to felt fabric. Press felted piece flat, then cut out a 25 cm diameter circle.

EDGING

With RS facing, using 3.00mm (US C2) crochet hook and yarn B, inserting hook through fabric of centre section approx 5 mm from cut edge, work around entire outer edge of centre section as folls: (1 dc into centre section, 1 ch) 100 times, ss to first dc. 200 sts.

Now work edging as folls:

Round 1 (RS): 3 ch (counts as 1 tr), miss st at base of 3 ch, 1 tr into each ch sp and dc to end, ss to top of 3 ch at beg of round. 200 sts.

Round 2: 1 ch (does NOT count as st), 1 dc into each of first 3 tr, *2 ch, miss 1 tr, (2 tr, 2 ch and 2 tr) into next tr, 2 ch, miss 1 tr**, 1 dc into each of next 5 tr, rep from * to end, ending last rep at **, 1 dc into each of last 2 tr, ss to first dc. 25 patt reps.

Round 3: 1 ch (does NOT count as st), 1 dc into each of first 2 dc, *3 ch, miss (1 dc, 2 ch and 2 tr), (3 tr, 2 ch and 3 tr) into next ch sp, 3 ch, miss (2 tr, 2 ch and 1 dc)**, 1 dc into each of next 3 dc, rep from * to end, ending last rep at **, 1 dc into last dc, ss to first dc.

Round 4: 1 ch (does NOT count as st), 1 dc into first dc, *4 ch, miss (1 dc, 3 ch and 3 tr), (4 tr, 2 ch and 4 tr) into next ch sp, 4 ch, miss (3 tr, 3 ch and 1 dc), 1 dc into next dc, rep from * to end, replacing dc at end of last rep with ss to first dc.

Round 5: 1 ch (does NOT count as st), 1 dc into first dc, *6 ch, miss (4 ch and 4 tr), (4 tr, 2 ch and 4 tr) into next ch sp, 6 ch, miss (4 tr and 4 ch), 1 dc into next dc, rep from * to end, replacing dc at end of last rep with ss to first dc.

Fasten off.

MAKING UP

Press as described on the information page.

garter stitch pouffe 

main image page 13

YARN

Rowan Purelife Renew

A	Garage	684	25	x 50gm
B	Camper	690	5	x 50gm
C	Mini	688	5	x 50gm
D	Trailer	681	5	x 50gm
E	Pick Up	683	5	x 50gm
F	Diesel	685	5	x 50gm

NEEDLES

1 pair 10mm (no 000) (US 15) needles

EXTRAS - 80 cm diameter pouffe, 20 cm tall

TENSION

10 sts and 17 rows to 10 cm measured over g st using 10mm (US 15) needles and yarn DOUBLE.

CIRCLES (make 2)

Using 10mm (US 15) needles and yarn A DOUBLE cast on 40 sts.

Row 1 (WS): sl 1, K to end.

Row 2: K38, wrap next st (by slipping next st from left needle to right needle, taking yarn to opposite side of work between needles, then slipping same st back onto left needle - when working back across wrapped sts, work the wrapped st and the wrapping loop tog as 1 st) and turn.

Row 3 and every foll alt row: Knit.

Row 4: K37, wrap next st and turn.

Row 6: K36, wrap next st and turn.

Row 8: K35, wrap next st and turn.

Row 10: K34, wrap next st and turn.

Row 12: K33, wrap next st and turn.

Row 14: K32, wrap next st and turn.

Row 16: K31, wrap next st and turn.

Row 18: K30, wrap next st and turn.

Cont in this way, working one less st on every RS row before wrapping next st and turning, until the foll row has been worked:

Row 72 (RS): K3, wrap next st and turn.

Row 73: Knit.

Break off yarn A and join in yarn B DOUBLE.

Next row (RS): K across all 40 sts.

Now rep rows 1 to 73 once more.

Break off yarn B and join in yarn C DOUBLE.

Next row (RS): K across all 40 sts.

Now rep rows 1 to 73 once more.

Break off yarn C and join in yarn D DOUBLE.

Next row (RS): K across all 40 sts.

Now rep rows 1 to 73 once more.

Break off yarn D and join in yarn E DOUBLE.

Next row (RS): K across all 40 sts.

Now rep rows 1 to 73 once more.

Break off yarn E and join in yarn F DOUBLE.

Next row (RS): K across all 40 sts.

Now rep rows 1 to 73 once more.

Cast off all sts.

SIDE PANEL

Using 10mm (US 15) needles and yarn A DOUBLE cast on 21 sts.

Work in g st until work meas 252 cm, ending with **RS** facing for next row.

Cast off.

MAKING UP

Press as described on the information page.

Sew cast-off edge of circle to cast-on edge to complete the circle. Join cast-on and cast-off edges of side panel to form a loop. Now sew one row-end edge of side panel to outer row-end edge of one circle. Sew other circle to other row-end edge of side panel, enclosing pouffe inside knitted sections.

garter stitch rug or throw

main image page 14

YARN
Rowan Purelife British Sheep Breeds Bouclé & Purelife British Sheep Breeds Chunky
A Bouclé
Mid Brown Masham

222	14	x 100gm

B Chunky
Steel Grey Suffolk

954	8	x 100gm

NEEDLES
20mm (US 36) circular needle

EXTRAS - For rug, piece of firm backing fabric (such as calico or hessian) 140 cm by 190 cm

TENSION
5 sts and 10 rows to 10 cm measured over g st using 20mm (US 36) needles and yarn DOUBLE.

FINISHED SIZE
Completed rug/throw measures 120 cm (47 ins) by 180 cm (71 ins).

RUG/THROW
Using 20mm (US 36) circular needle and yarn A DOUBLE cast on 60 sts.
Now work in striped g st as folls:
Rows 1 and 2: Using yarn A DOUBLE, knit.
Join in yarn B DOUBLE.
Rows 3 and 4: Using yarn B DOUBLE, knit.
These 4 rows form striped g st.
Cont in striped g st until work meas approx 180 cm, ending after 2 rows using yarn A DOUBLE.
Cast off.

MAKING UP
Press as described on the information page.
If using as a rug, trim backing fabric to same size as knitted section, adding 1.5 cm along all edges. Turn under these edges, lay fabric against WS of rug and neatly sew in place.

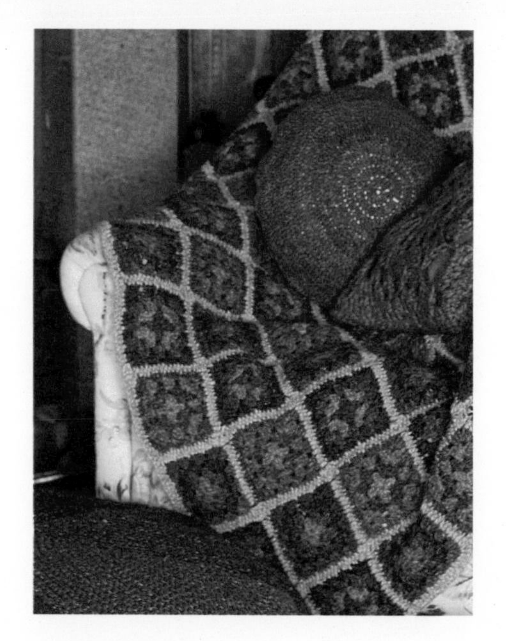

granny squares throw 

main image page 24

YARN

Rowan Purelife Renew

A	Mini	688	4	x 50gm
B	Trailer	681	9	x 50gm
C	Camper	690	5	x 50gm
D	Pick Up	683	10	x 50gm
E	Diesel	685	4	x 50gm
F	Digger	682	4	x 50gm
G	Garage	684	5	x 50gm
H	Tractor	680	9	x 50gm

CROCHET HOOK

6.00mm (no 4) (US J10) crochet hook

TENSION

Basic motif meas 12 cm square using 6.00mm (US J10) crochet hook.

FINISHED SIZE

Completed throw measures 136 cm (53½ ins) by 177 cm (69 1/2 ins).

CROCHET ABBREVIATIONS

ch = chain; **sp(s)** = space(s); **ss** = slip stitch; **tr** = treble.

BASIC MOTIF

Using 6.00mm (US J10) hook and first colour make 4 ch and join with a ss to form a ring.

Joining in and breaking off colours as required, cont as folls:

Round 1 (RS): Using first colour, 5 ch (counts as 1 tr and 2 ch), (3 tr into ring, 2 ch) 3 times, 2 tr into ring, ss to 3rd of 5 ch at beg of round.

Round 2: Using 2nd colour, ss into first ch sp, 5 ch (counts as 1 tr and 2 ch), 3 tr into ch sp at base of 5 ch, *1 ch, miss 3 tr, (3 tr, 2 ch and 3 tr) into next ch sp, rep from * twice more, 1 ch, miss 3 tr, 2 tr into same ch sp as used at beg of round, ss to 3rd of 5 ch at beg of round.

Round 3: Using 3rd colour, ss into first ch sp, 5 ch (counts as 1 tr and 2 ch), 3 tr into ch sp at base of 5 ch, *1 ch, miss 3 tr, 3 tr into next ch sp, 1 ch, miss 3 tr**, (3 tr, 2 ch and 3 tr) into next ch sp, rep from * to end, ending last rep at **, 2 tr into same ch sp as used at beg of round, ss to 3rd of 5 ch at beg of round.

Round 4: Using 4th colour, ss into first ch sp, 5 ch (counts as 1 tr and 2 ch), 3 tr into ch sp at base of 5 ch, *(1 ch, miss 3 tr, 3 tr into next ch sp) twice, 1 ch, miss 3 tr**, (3 tr, 2 ch and 3 tr) into next ch sp, rep from * to end, ending last rep at **, 2 tr into same ch sp as used at beg of round, ss to 3rd of 5 ch at beg of round.

Fasten off.

Completed basic motif is a square. In each corner there is a 2-ch sp and along each side, between the corner ch sps, there are 4 groups of 3 tr, each separated by a 1-ch sp. 17 sts (12 tr and 5 ch) along each side of motif.

THROW

Using colours as folls, make 130 basic motifs:

Motif A (make 44)

First colour: yarn A, 2nd colour: yarn B, 3rd colour: yarn C, 4th colour: yarn D.

Motif B (make 43)

First colour: yarn C, 2nd colour: yarn D, 3rd colour: yarn E, 4th colour: yarn B.

Motif C (make 43)

First colour: yarn F, 2nd colour: yarn A, 3rd colour: yarn D, 4th colour: yarn G.

Join motifs into strips

Following diagram, join motifs into strips as folls: With RS facing, 6.00mm (US J10) hook and yarn

A	B	C	A	B	C	A	B	C	A	B	C	A
B	C	A	B	C	A	B	C	A	B	C	A	B
C	A	B	C	A	B	C	A	B	C	A	B	C
A	B	C	A	B	C	A	B	C	A	B	C	A
B	C	A	B	C	A	B	C	A	B	C	A	B
C	A	B	C	A	B	C	A	B	C	A	B	C
A	B	C	A	B	C	A	B	C	A	B	C	A
B	C	A	B	C	A	B	C	A	B	C	A	B
C	A	B	C	A	B	C	A	B	C	A	B	C
A	B	C	A	B	C	A	B	C	A	B	C	A

H, attach yarn to corner ch sp of first motif, 3 ch (counts as 1 tr), holding RS of next motif against RS of first motif, work 1 ss into corresponding corner ch sp of 2nd motif, *(1 tr into next tr of first motif, 1 ss into corresponding tr of 2nd motif) 3 times, 1 tr into next ch sp of first motif, 1 ss into corresponding ch sp of 2nd motif, rep from * until tr and ss have been worked into corner ch sps at other end of this edge of motifs.

Fasten off.

Following diagram, cont to join motifs to form 13 strips of 10 motifs.

Join strips

Following diagram, join strips into one large rectangle as folls:

With RS facing, 6.00mm (US J10) hook and yarn H, attach yarn to corner ch sp of end motif of first strip, 3 ch (counts as 1 tr), holding RS of end motif of next strip against RS of end motif of first strip, work 1 ss into correspond corner ch sp of 2nd strip motif, *(1 tr into next tr of first motif, 1 ss into correspond tr of 2nd motif) 3 times, 1 tr into next ch sp of first motif, 1 ss into corresponding ch sp of 2nd motif, rep from * until tr and ss have been worked into corner ch sps at other end of this edge of first pair of motifs, now join strips across row joining motifs as folls: (1 tr around stem of tr joining first strip, 1 ss around corresponding tr joining 2nd strip) twice, cont in this way until all 10 motifs of strips are joined.

Fasten off.

Edging

With RS facing, 6.00mm (US J10) hook and yarn H, attach yarn along one side of joined motifs, 3 ch (counts as 1 tr), miss st at base of 3 ch, now work one round of tr around entire outer edge of joined motifs, working 1 tr into each tr and ch sp along edges of motifs, 2 tr around stem of tr joining motifs and strips, and 3 tr into ch sps at corners, and ending with ss to top of 3 ch at beg of round.

Fasten off.

Press as described on the information page.

crochet squares cushion

main image page 24

YARN

Rowan Purelife Renew

5 x 50gm

(photographed in Garage 684, Camper 690 & Pickup 683)

CROCHET HOOK

15mm (US P19) crochet hook

EXTRAS - 38 cm (15 in) square cushion pad and 45 cm by 90 cm piece of lining fabric

TENSION

Basic motif meas 38 cm square using 15mm (US P19) crochet hook and yarn DOUBLE.

CROCHET ABBREVIATIONS

ch = chain; **dc** = double crochet; **sp(s)** = space(s); **ss** = slip stitch; **tr** = treble.

FRONT and BACK (both alike)

Remembering to use yarn DOUBLE, make 2 motifs as given for crochet squares throw - one will be front, other will be back.

MAKING UP

Press as described on the information page.

From lining fabric, cut two 41 cm squares. Taking 1.5 cm seam allowance, sew these squares together along 3 sides. Turn RS out and insert cushion pad. Fold in seam allowance along rem side and close this 4th side.

Join front and back along all 4 sides, inserting covered cushion pad before closing 4th side.

graphic squares cushion 

main image page 29

YARN

Rowan Purelife Renew

A Mini	688	2	x 50gm
B Trailer	681	2	x 50gm
C Camper	690	1	x 50gm
D Pick Up	683	2	x 50gm
E Garage	684	1	x 50gm

NEEDLES

1 pair 6mm (no 4) (US 10) needles

EXTRAS - 35 cm (14 in) by 56 cm (22 in) cushion pad

TENSION

14 sts and 20 rows to 10 cm measured over patterned st st using 6mm (US 10) needles.

FRONT and BACK (both alike)

Using 6mm (US 10) needles and yarn A cast on 78 sts.

Joining in and breaking off colours as required and using the intarsia technique as described on the information page, now work in patt as folls:

Row 1 (RS): Using yarn A K13, using yarn B K12, using yarn C K8, using yarn D K12, using yarn E K12, using yarn A K8, using yarn B K13.

Row 2: Using yarn B P13, using yarn A P8, using yarn E P12, using yarn D P12, using yarn C P8, using yarn B P12, using yarn A P13.

Rows 3 to 24: As rows 1 and 2, 11 times.

Row 25: Using yarn E K13, using yarn D K12, using yarn A K8, using yarn B K12, using yarn C K12, using yarn D K8, using yarn E K13.

Row 26: Using yarn E P13, using yarn D P8, using yarn C P12, using yarn B P12, using yarn A P8, using yarn D P12, using yarn E P13.

Rows 27 to 46: As rows 25 and 26, 10 times.

Row 47: Using yarn B K13, using yarn C K12, using yarn D K8, using yarn E K12, using yarn A K12, using yarn B K8, using yarn D K13.

Row 48: Using yarn D P13, using yarn B P8, using yarn A P12, using yarn E P12, using yarn D P8, using yarn C P12, using yarn B P13.

Rows 49 to 70: As rows 47 and 48, 11 times.

Cast off.

MAKING UP

Press as described on the information page.

Join front and back along all 4 sides, inserting cushion pad before closing 4th side.

lattice spot cushion

main image page 21

YARN

Rowan Purelife British Sheep Breeds Chunky and Purelife British Sheep Breeds Bouclé

A Chunky	Lt Masham
957 2	x 100gm
B Chunky	Mid Brown Jacob
952 1	x 100gm
C Chunky	Black Welsh
951 1	x 100gm
D Bouclé	Lt Brown Masham
221 2	x 100gm

NEEDLES

1 pair 7mm (no 2) (US 10½) needles

EXTRAS - 45 cm (18 in) square cushion pad

TENSION

13 sts and 18 rows to 10 cm measured over patterned st st using 7mm (US 10 1/2) needles.

FRONT and BACK (both alike)

Using 7mm (US 10½) needles and yarn A cast on 59 sts.

Using the **intarsia** technique as described on the information page, now work in patt from chart, which is worked entirely in st st beg with a K row, as folls:

Work all 24 rows of chart 3 times, then rep chart rows 1 to 8 once more, ending with RS facing for next row.

Cast off.

MAKING UP

Press as described on the information page.

Join front and back along all 4 sides, inserting cushion pad before closing 4th side.

key

- ☐ A
- ☒ B
- O C
- | D

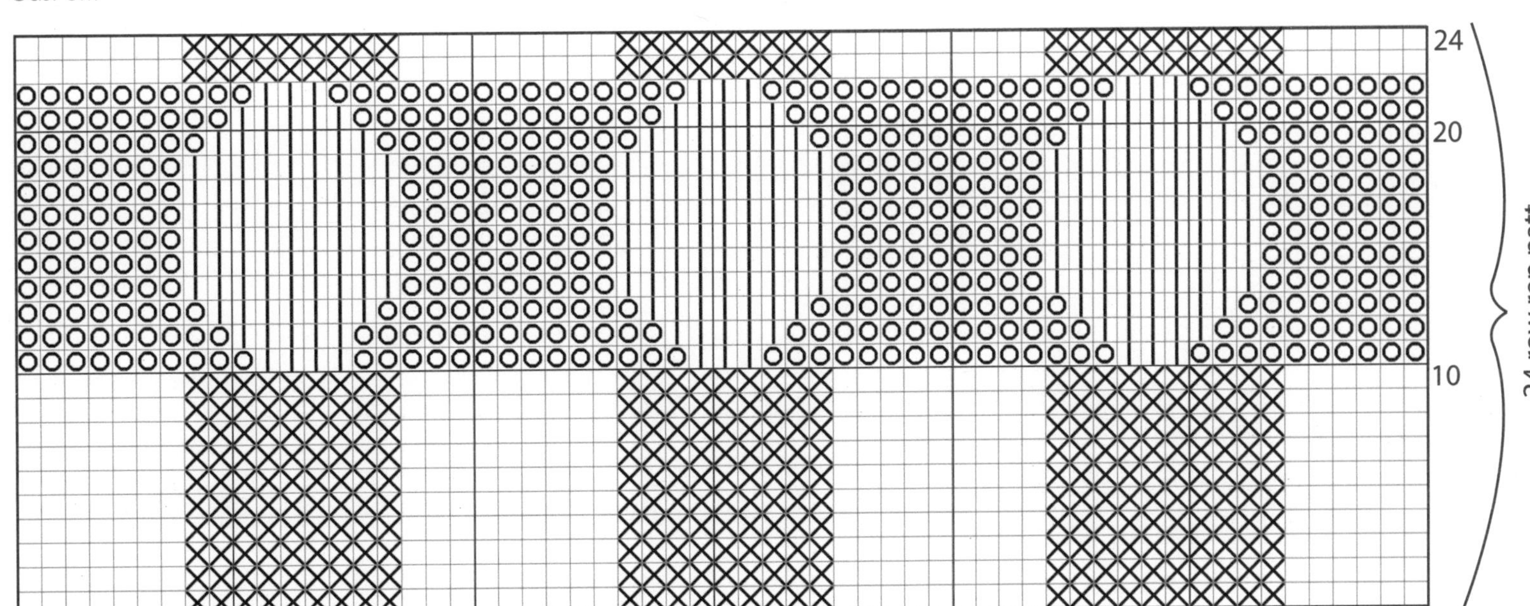

mini graphics cushion 

main image page 19

YARN
Rowan Purelife British Sheep Breeds DK

A Bluefaced Leicester
780 2 x 50gm

B Mid Brown Bluefaced Leicester
782 2 x 50gm

C Brown Bluefaced Leicester
781 2 x 50gm

NEEDLES
1 pair 3¼mm (no 10) (US 3) needles

EXTRAS - 33 cm (13 in) by 43 cm (17 in) cushion pad

TENSION
28 sts and 27 rows to 10 cm measured over patterned st st using 3¼mm (US 3) needles.

FRONT and BACK (both alike)
Using 3¼ mm (US 3) needles and yarn A cast on 92 sts.
Using the **intarsia** technique as described on the information page, now work in patt from chart, which is worked entirely in st st beg with a K row, as folls:
Work all 57 rows of chart, ending with **WS** facing for next row.
Now, noting that this rep of chart will beg with a **purl** row, rep all 57 rows of chart once more, ending with RS facing for next row.
Now, noting that this rep of chart will beg with a **knit** row, rep chart rows 1 to 3 once more, ending with **WS** facing for next row.
Cast off (on **WS**).

MAKING UP
Press as described on the information page.
Join front and back along all 4 sides, inserting cushion pad before closing 4th side.

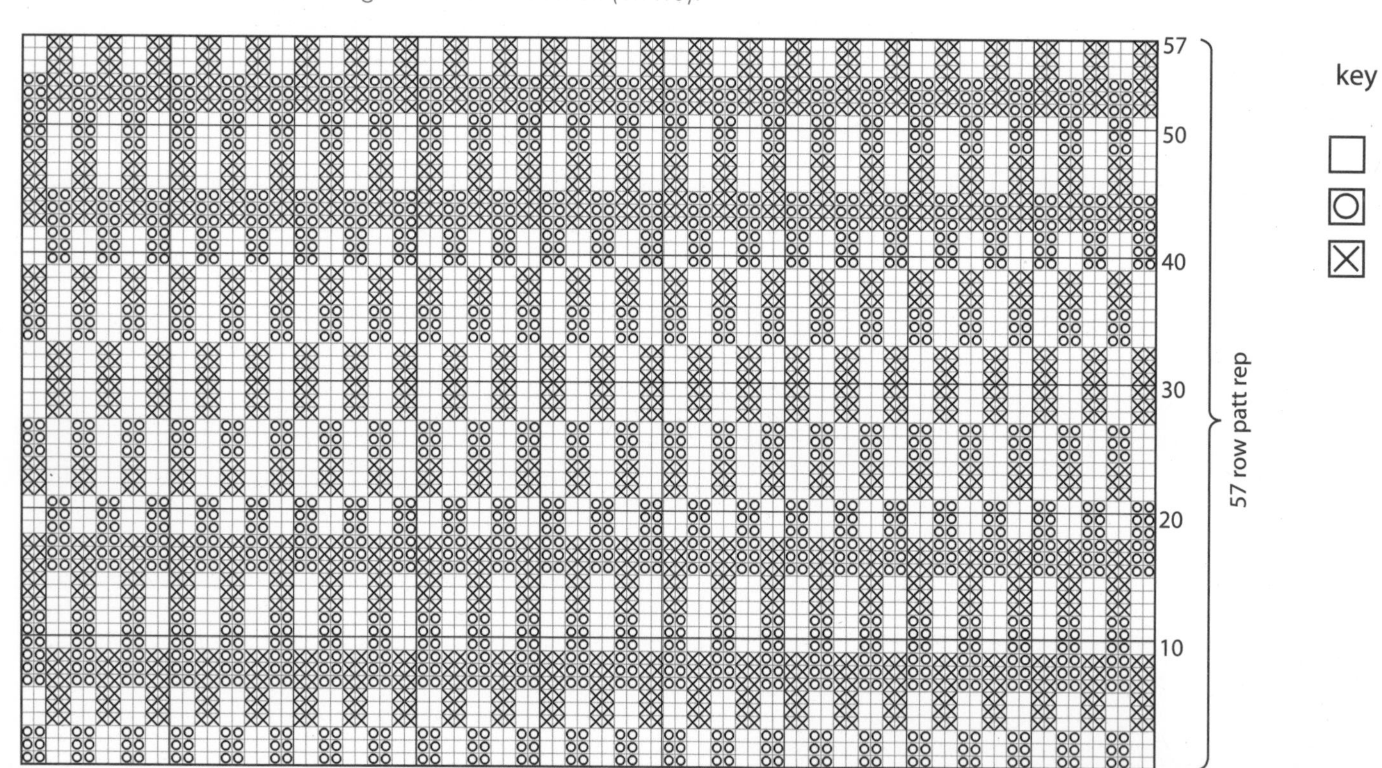

key

- ☐ A
- ◯ B
- ☒ C

plaited place mat

main image page 22

YARN

Rowan Purelife Renew

A Camper	690	3	x 50gm
B Pick Up	683	3	x 50gm
C Mini	688	3	x 50gm

CROCHET HOOK

6.00mm (no 4) (US J10) crochet hook

TENSION

Completed plait should be approx 310 cm long and 2 cm wide.

FINISHED SIZE

Completed place mat measures 30 cm (12 ins) in diameter.

CROCHET ABBREVIATIONS

ch = chain; **dc** = double crochet.

PLACE MAT

Using 6.00mm (US J10) hook and yarn A make 560 ch.

Row 1 (RS): 1 dc into 2nd ch from hook, 1 dc into each ch to end.

Fasten off.

Make a further 2 strips in same way - one using yarn B and one using yarn C.

Join ends of strips together and then plait the 3 strips together to form a plait approx 310 cm long and 2 cm wide. When complete, secure ends.

Now, using photograph as a guide, wind the plait into a spiral to create place mat - sew edges of plait together on WS as you go and secure ends.

Press as described on the information page.

textured rug

main image page 6

YARN

Rowan Purelife British Sheep Breeds Boucle & Purelife British Sheep Breeds Chunky

A Chunky	Lt Masham		
957	6	x 100gm	
B Boucle	Mid Brown Masham		
222	7	x 100gm	
C Chunky	Black Welsh		
951	2	x 100gm	
D Chunky	Shetland Moorit		
955	4	x 100gm	
E Boucle	Lt Brown Masham		
221	2	x 100gm	
F Boucle	Dark Brown Masham		
227	7	x 100gm	

NEEDLES

20mm (US 36) circular needle

EXTRAS - Piece of firm backing fabric (such as calico or hessian) 130 cm by 190 cm

TENSION

5 sts and 7 rows to 10 cm measured over st st using 20mm (US 36) needles and 3 strands of chunky yarn held together.

FINISHED SIZE

Completed rug measures 120 cm (47 ins) by 174 cm (68½ ins).

SPECIAL ABBREVIATIONS

ML = make loop as folls: K next st leaving st on left needle, bring yarn to front of work and wrap it under, round and over left thumb forming a loop approx 4 cm long, take yarn back to WS of work, K st on left needle again and let st drop off left needle, yfwd, now lift 2nd and 3rd sts on right needle over first st (the yfwd) and off right needle.

Pattern note: When using chunky yarn, use **THREE** strands held together throughout, but when using boucle yarn use **TWO** strands held together throughout.

RUG

Using 20mm (US 36) circular needle and 3 strands of yarn A held together cast on 60 sts.
Row 1 (RS): *K1, P1, rep from * to end.
Row 2: *P1, K1, rep from * to end.
These 2 rows form moss st.
Cont in moss st until work meas 20 cm, ending with RS facing for next row.
Next row (RS): Purl.
Break off yarn A and join in yarn B DOUBLE.
Now work in fur st patt as folls:
Row 1 (WS): Knit.
Row 2: *K1, ML, rep from * to last 2 sts, K2.
Row 3: Knit.
Row 4: K2, *Ml, K1, rep from * to end.
These 4 rows form fur st patt.
Cont in fur st patt until work meas 50 cm, ending with RS facing for next row.
Break off yarn B and join in 3 strands of yarn C held together.
Beg with a K row, work in st st for 8 rows, ending with RS facing for next row.
Break off yarn C and join in 3 strands of yarn D held together.
Work in g st for 6 rows, ending with RS facing for next row.
Break off yarn C and join in yarn E DOUBLE.
Beg with a K row, work in st st for 6 rows, ending with RS facing for next row.
Break off yarn E and join in 3 strands of yarn A held together.
Now work in rib as folls:
Row 1 (RS): *K3, P3, rep from * to end.
Row 2: As row 1.
These 2 rows form rib.
Cont in rib until work meas 12 cm from beg of rib, ending with RS facing for next row.
Next row (RS): Purl.
Break off yarn A.
Using yarn F DOUBLE and 3 strands of yarn D held together, now work in checkerboard patt as folls:
Row 1 (WS): *Using F K6, using D K6, rep from * to end.
Row 2: *Using D K6, using F (K1, ML) twice, K2, rep from * to end.
Row 3: As row 1.
Row 4: *Using D K6, using F K2, (ML, K1) twice, rep from * to end.
Rows 5 to 8: As rows 1 to 4.
Row 9: *Using D K6, using F K6, rep from * to end.
Row 10: *Using F (K1, ML) twice, K2, using D K6, rep from * to end.
Row 11: As row 9.
Row 12: *Using F K2, (ML, K1) twice, using D K6, rep from * to end.
Rows 13 to 16: As rows 9 to 12.
These 16 rows form checkerboard patt.
Work in checkerboard patt for a further 25 rows, ending with RS facing for next row.
Break off yarns D and F and join in 3 strands of yarn A held together.
Beg with a K row, work in st st for 4 rows, ending with RS facing for next row.
Break off yarn A and join in yarn B DOUBLE.
Next row (RS): Knit.
Beg with a K row, work in rev st st for 3 rows, ending with RS facing for next row.
Break off yarn B and join in 3 strands of yarn A held together.
Beg with a K row, work in st st for 4 rows, ending

with RS facing for next row.
Break off yarn A and join in yarn F DOUBLE.
Next row (RS): Knit.
Beg with a K row, work in rev st st for 3 rows, ending with RS facing for next row.
Break off yarn F and join in 3 strands of yarn A held together.
Beg with a K row, work in st st for 4 rows, ending with RS facing for next row.
Break off yarn A and join in yarn E DOUBLE.
Next row (RS): Knit.
Beg with a K row, work in rev st st for 3 rows, ending with RS facing for next row.
Cast off.

MAKING UP
Press as described on the information page.
Trim backing fabric to same size as knitted section, adding 1.5 cm along all edges. Turn under these edges, lay fabric against WS of rug and neatly sew in place.

tweed throw

main image page 8

YARN
Rowan Purelife Renew

A Trailer	681	7	x 50gm
B Garage	684	5	x 50gm
C Pick Up	683	5	x 50gm
D Camper	690	5	x 50gm
E Mini	688	5	x 50gm
F Diesel	685	2	x 50gm
G Digger	682	3	x 50gm

NEEDLES
6mm (no 4) (US 10) circular needle

TENSION
17 sts and 27 rows to 10 cm measured over tweed patt A using 6mm (US 10) needles.

FINISHED SIZE
Completed throw measures 120 cm (47 ins) by 160 cm (63 ins).

SPECIAL ABBREVIATIONS
ytb = take yarn to back (WS on RS rows, or RS on WS rows) of work; **ytf** = bring yarn to front (RS on RS rows, or WS on WS rows) of work.

THROW
Using 6mm (US 10) circular needle and yarn A cast on 191 sts.
Row 1 (RS): K1, *P1, K1, rep from * to end.
Row 2: As row 1.
These 2 rows form moss st.
Work in moss st for a further 7 rows, ending with WS facing for next row.
Row 10 (WS): Knit.
Break off yarn A.
Join in and breaking off colours as required, now work in tweed patts as folls:
First tweed patt A band
Now work in tweed patt A as folls:
Row 1 (RS): Using yarn B, knit.
Row 2: Using yarn B, P1, ytb, sl 1, ytf, *P3, ytb, sl 1, ytf, rep from * to last st, P1.
Row 3: Using yarn B, K1, sl 1, *K3, sl 1, rep from * to last st, K1.
Row 4: Using yarn C, P3, *ytb, sl 1, ytf, P3, rep from * to end.
Row 5: Using yarn C, K3, *sl 1, K3, rep from * to end.
Rows 6 and 7: As rows 2 and 3 **but** using yarn D.
Rows 8 and 9: As rows 4 and 5 **but** using yarn B.
Rows 10 and 11: As rows 2 and 3 **but** using yarn C.
Rows 12 and 13: As rows 4 and 5 **but** using yarn D.
Rows 14 to 73: As rows 2 to 13, 5 times.
Rows 74 and 75: As rows 2 and 3.
Row 76 (WS): Using yarn B, purl.
This completes first band in tweed patt A.
First tweed patt B band
Now work in tweed patt B as folls:

Row 1 (RS): Using yarn A, knit.
Row 2: Using yarn A, P1, ytb, sl 1, ytf, *P3, ytb, sl 1, ytf, rep from * to last st, P1.
Row 3: Using yarn A, K1, sl 1, *K3, sl 1, rep from * to last st, K1.
Row 4: Using yarn E, P3, *ytb, sl 1, ytf, P3, rep from * to end.
Row 5: Using yarn E, K3, *sl 1, K3, rep from * to end.
Rows 6 to 37: As rows 2 to 5, 8 times.
Rows 38 and 39: As rows 2 and 3.
Row 40 (WS): Using yarn A, purl.
This completes first band in tweed patt B.

Second tweed patt A band
Using yarn F instead of yarn B, yarn D instead of yarn C and yarn C instead of yarn D, work rows 1 to 13 as given for first tweed patt A band.
Rep last 8 rows once more, then work rows 74 to 76.

Second tweed patt B band
Using yarn G instead of yarn A, work rows 1 to 5 as given for first tweed patt B band.
Rep last 4 rows 14 times more, then work rows 46 to 48.

Third tweed patt A band
Work rows 1 to 13 as given for first tweed patt A band.
Rep last 8 rows twice more, then work rows 74 to 76.

Third tweed patt B band
Work rows 1 to 5 as given for first tweed patt B band.
Rep last 4 rows 5 times more, then work rows 46 to 48.

Fourth tweed patt A band
Using yarn F instead of yarn B, yarn D instead of yarn C and yarn C instead of yarn D, work rows 1 to 13 as given for first tweed patt A band.
Rep last 8 rows once more, then work rows 74 to 76.

Fourth tweed patt B band
Using yarn G instead of yarn A, work rows 1 to 5 as given for first tweed patt B band.
Rep last 4 rows 5 times more, then work rows 46 to 48.

Fifth tweed patt A band
Work rows 1 to 13 as given for first tweed patt A band.
Rep last 12 rows 5 times more, then work rows 74 to 76.
Break off yarns B, C and D and join in yarn A.
Next row (RS): Knit.
Work in moss st as given for cast-on edge for 9 rows, ending with RS facing for next row.
Cast off in moss st.

MAKING UP
Press as described on the information page.

Side borders (both alike)
With RS facing, using 6mm (US 10) circular needle and yarn A, pick up and knit 289 sts evenly along one entire row-end edge, between cast-on and cast-off edges.
Work in moss st as given for cast-on edge for 9 rows, ending with RS facing for next row.
Cast off in moss st.

two tone stripe cushion

main image page 19

YARN
Rowan Purelife British Sheep Breeds DK
A Mid Brown Bluefaced Leicester
782 1 x 50gm
B Bluefaced Leicester
780 1 x 50gm
C Brown Bluefaced Leicester
781 3 x 50gm

NEEDLES
1 pair 3¼mm (no 10) (US 3) needles

EXTRAS - 35 cm (14 in) square cushion pad

TENSION
26 sts and 33 rows to 10 cm measured over st st using 3¼mm (US 3) needles.

FRONT and BACK (both alike)
Using 3¼mm (US 3) needles and yarn A cast on 90 sts.
Beg with a K row, work in st st for 49 rows, ending with **WS** facing for next row.
Using the **intarsia** technique as described on the information page, now work in patt from chart, which is worked entirely in st st beg with a **purl** row, as folls:
Work all 14 rows of chart, ending with **WS** facing for next row.
Break off contrasts and cont using yarn C **only**.
Beg with a P row, work in st st for 49 rows, ending with RS facing for next row.
Cast off.

MAKING UP
Press as described on the information page.
Join front and back along all 4 sides, inserting cushion pad before closing 4th side.

key

☐ A
⊙ B
☒ C

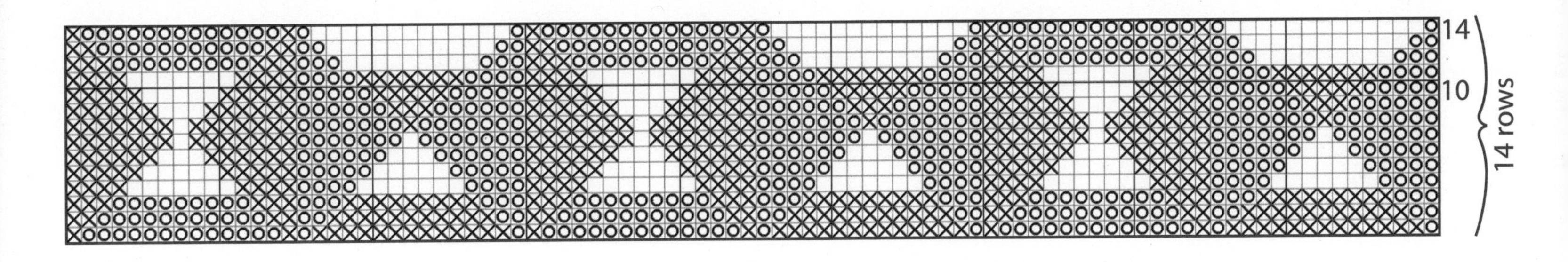

Tension

Obtaining the correct tension is perhaps the single factor which can make the difference between a successful garment and a disastrous one. It controls both the shape and size of an article, so any variation, however slight, can distort the finished garment. Different designers feature in our books and it is their tension, given at the start of each pattern, which you must match. We recommend that you knit a square in pattern and/or stocking stitch (depending on the pattern instructions) of perhaps 5 – 10 more stitches and 5 – 10 more rows than those given in the tension note. Mark out the central 10cm square with pins. If you have too many stitches to 10cm try again using thicker needles, if you have too few stitches to 10cm try again using finer needles. Once you have achieved the correct tension your garment will be knitted to the measurements indicated in the size diagram shown at the end of the pattern.

Chart Note

Many of the patterns in the book are worked from charts. Each square on a chart represents a stitch and each line of squares a row of knitting. Each colour used is given a different letter and these are shown in the materials section, or in the key alongside the chart of each pattern.
When working from the charts, read odd rows (K) from right to left and even rows (P) from left to right, unless otherwise stated.

Knitting With Colour

There are two main methods of working colour into a knitted fabric: Intarsia and Fairisle techniques. The first method produces a single thickness of fabric and is usually used where a colour is only required in a particular area of a row and does not form a repeating pattern across the row, as in the fairisle technique.
Intarsia: The simplest way to do this is to cut short lengths of yarn for each motif or block of colour used in a row. Then joining in the various colours at the appropriate point on the row, link one colour to the next by twisting them around each other where they meet on the wrong side to avoid gaps. All ends can then either be darned along the colour join lines, as each motif is completed or then can be "knitted-in" to the fabric of the knitting as each colour is worked into the pattern. This is done in much the same way as "weaving- in" yarns when working the Fairisle technique and does save time darning-in ends. It is essential that the tension is noted for Intarsia as this may vary from the stocking stitch if both are used in the same pattern.
Fairisle type knitting: When two or three colours are worked repeatedly across a row, strand the yarn not in use loosely behind the stitches being worked. If you are working with more than two colours, treat the "floating" yarns as if they were one yarn and always spread the stitches to their correct width to keep them elastic. It is advisable not to carry the stranded or "floating" yarns over more than three stitches at a time, but to weave them under and over the colour you are working. The "floating" yarns are therefore caught at the back of the work.

Finishing Instructions

After working for hours knitting a garment, it seems a great pity that many garments are spoiled because such little care is taken in the pressing and finishing process. Follow the following tips for a truly professional looking garment.

Pressing

Block out each piece of knitting and following the instructions on the ball band press the garment pieces, omitting the ribs.

Tip

Take special care to press the edges, as this will make sewing up both easier and neater. If the ball band indicates that the fabric is not to be pressed, then covering the blocked out fabric with a damp white cotton cloth and leaving it to stand will have the desired effect. Darn in all ends neatly along the selvage edge or a colour join, as appropriate.

Stitching

When stitching the pieces together, remember to match areas of colour and texture very carefully where they meet. Use a seam stitch such as back stitch or mattress stitch for all main
knitting seams and join all ribs and neckband with mattress stitch, unless otherwise stated.

Experience Ratings

Easy, straight forward knitting

Suitable for the average knitter

Suitable for the more experienced knitter

Abbreviations

K	knit
P	purl
st(s)	stitch(es)
inc	increas(e)(ing)
dec	decreas(e)(ing)
st st	stocking stitch (1 row K, 1 row P)
g st	garter stitch (K every row)
beg	begin(ning)
foll	following
rem	remain(ing)
rev st st	reverse stocking stitch (1 row K, 1row P)
rep	repeat
alt	alternate
cont	continue
patt	pattern
tog	together
mm	millimetres
cm	centimetres
in(s)	inch(es)
RS	right side
WS	wrong side
sl 1	slip one stitch
psso	pass slipped stitch over
p2sso	pass 2 slipped stitches over
tbl	through back of loop
M1	make one stitch by picking up horizontal loop before next stitch and knitting into back of it
M1P	make one stitch by picking up horizontal loop before next stitch and purling into back of it
yfwd	yarn forward
yrn	yarn round needle
meas	measures
0	no stitches, times or rows
-	no stitches, times or rows for that size
yon	yarn over needle
yfrn	yarn forward round needle
wyib	with yarn at back

Crochet Terms

UK crochet terms and abbreviations have been used throughout. The list below gives the US equivalent where they vary.

ABBREV.

	UK	US
dc	double crochet	single crochet
htr	half treble	half double crochet
tr	treble	double crochet
dtr	double treble	treble
ttr	triple treble	double treble
qtr	quadruple treble	triple treble

stockists

AUSTRALIA: Australian Country Spinners Pty Ltd, Level 7, 409 St. Kilda Road, Melbourne 3004. Tel: 03 9380 3830 Email: tkohut@auspinners.com.au

AUSTRIA: Coats Harlander GmbH, Autokaderstrasse 31, Wien A -1210. Tel: (01) 27716

BELGIUM: Coats Benelux, Ring Oost 14A, Ninove, 9400 Tel: 054 318989 Email: sales.coatsninove@coats.com

CANADA: Westminster Fibers, 8 Shelter Drive, Greer, South Carolina, 29650 Tel: 800 445-9276 Email: info@westminsterfibers.com Web: www.westminsterfibers.com

CHINA: Coats Shanghai Ltd, No 9 Building , Baosheng Road, Songjiang Industrial Zone, Shanghai. Tel: 86 21 5774 3733 Email: victor.li@coats.com

DENMARK: Coats HP A/S, Tagensvej 85C, St.tv., Copenhagen Tel: 45 35 86 90 49

FINLAND: Coats Opti Crafts Oy, Ketjutie 3, Kerava , 04220 Tel: (358) 9 274871 Email: coatsopti@coats.com Web: wwwcoatscrafts.fi

FRANCE: Coats Steiner, 100 Avenue du Général de Gaulle, Mehun-Sur-Yèvre, 18500 Tel: 02 48 23 12 30 Web: www.coatscrafts.fr

GERMANY: Coats GmbH, Kaiserstrasse 1, Kenzingen, 79341 Tel: 07162-14346 Web: www.coatsgmbh.de

HOLLAND: Coats Benelux, Ring Oost 14A, Ninove, 9400, Belgium Tel: 0346 35 37 00 Email: sales.coatsninove@coats.com

HONG KONG: Coats Shanghai Ltd, No 8 Building , Export & Processing Garden, Songjiang Industrial Zone, Shanghai, China. Tel: (86- 21) 57743733-326 Email: victor.li@coats.com

ICELAND: Rowan At Storkurinn, Laugavegur 59, Reykjavik, 101 Tel: 551 8258 Email: storkurinn@simnet.is Web: www.storkurinn.is

ISRAEL: Beit Hasidkit, Ms. Offra Tzenger, Sokolov St No 2, Kfar Sava, 44256 Tel: (972) 9 7482381

ITALY: Coats cucirini srl, Viale sarca no 223, Milano, 20126

KOREA: Coats Korea Co. Lt, 5F Eyeon B/D, 935-40 Bangbae-Dong, Seocho-Gu, Seoul, 137-060 Tel: 82-2-521-6262 Web: www.coatskorea.co.kr

LEBANON: y.knot, Saifi Village, Mkhalissiya Street 162, Beirut Tel: (961) 1 992211 Email: y.knot@cyberia.net.lb

LUXEMBOURG: Coats Benelux, Ring Oost 14A, Ninove, 9400, Belgium Tel: 0346 35 37 00 Email: sales.coatsninove@coats.com

MALTA: John Gregory Ltd, 8 Ta'Xbiex Sea Front, Msida, MSD 1512, Malta Tel: +356 2133 0202 Email: raygreg@onvol.net

NEW ZEALAND: ACS New Zealand, 1 March Place, Belfast, Christchurch Tel: 64-3-323-6665

NORWAY: Coats Knappehuset AS, Pb 100, Ulset, Bergen, 5873 Tel: 55 53 93 00

PORTUGAL: Coats & Clark, Quinta de Cravel, Apartado 444, Vila Nova de Gaia 4431-968 Tel: 223770700 Web: www.crafts.com.pt

SINGAPORE: Golden Dragon Store, 101 Upper Cross Street, #02-51, People's Park Centre, 058357, Singapore Tel: (65) 65358454/65358234 Email: gdscraft@hotmail.com

SOUTH AFRICA: Arthur Bales Ltd, 62 Fourth Avenue, Linden, Johannesburg, 2195 Tel: (27) 118 882 401 Email: arthurb@new.co.za Web: www.arthurbales.co.za

SPAIN: Coats Fabra, SA, Santa Adria, 20, Barcelona, 08030 Tel: (34) 93 290 84 00 Email: atencion.clientes@coats.com Web: www.coatscrafts.es

SWEDEN: Coats Expotex AB, JA Wettergrensgata 7, Vastra Frolunda, Goteborg, 431 30 Tel: (46) 33 720 79 00

SWITZERLAND: Coats Stroppel AG, Turgi (AG), CH-5300 Tel: 056 298 12 20

TAIWAN: Cactus Quality Co Ltd, 7FL-2, No. 140, Sec. 2 Roosevelt Road, Taipei, Taiwan, R.O.C. 10084 Tel: 00886-2-23656527 Email:cqcl@ms17.hinet.net Web: www.excelcraft.com.tw

THAILAND: Global Wide Trading, 10 Lad Prao Soi 88, Bangkok 10310 Tel: 00 662 933 9019 Email: TheNeedleWorld@yahoo.com – global.wide@yahoo.com

U.S.A.: Westminster Fibers Inc, 8 Shelter Drive, Greer, 29650, South Carolina Tel: (800) 445-9276 Email: info@westminsterfibers.com Web: www.westminsterfibers.com

U.K: Rowan, Green Lane Mill, Holmfirth, West Yorkshire, England HD9 2DX Tel: +44 (0) 1484 681881 Email: mail@knitrowan.com Web: www.knitrowan.com

For stockists in all other countries please contact Rowan for details

crochet doily rug
pattern page 35

dk striped and plain crochet circular cushions
pattern page 36

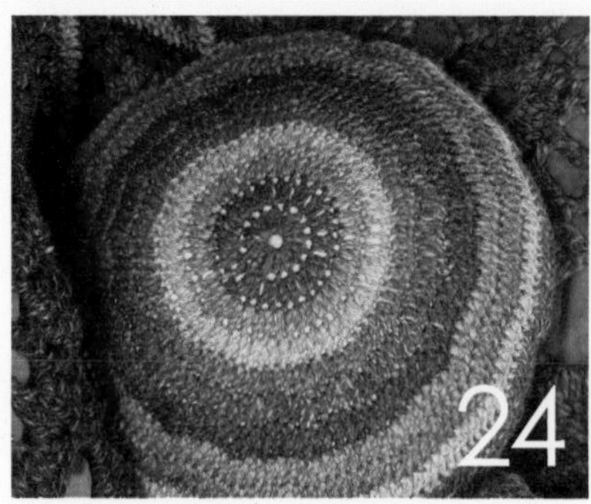

striped and plain crochet circular cushions
pattern page 37

crochet squares throw
pattern page 38

felted place mat
pattern page 39

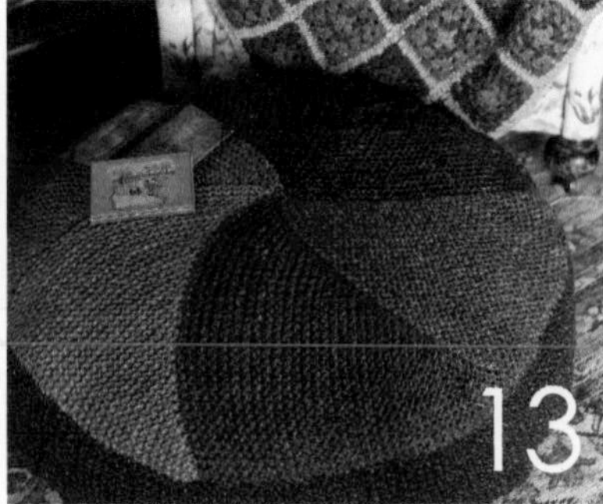

garter stitch pouffe
pattern page 40

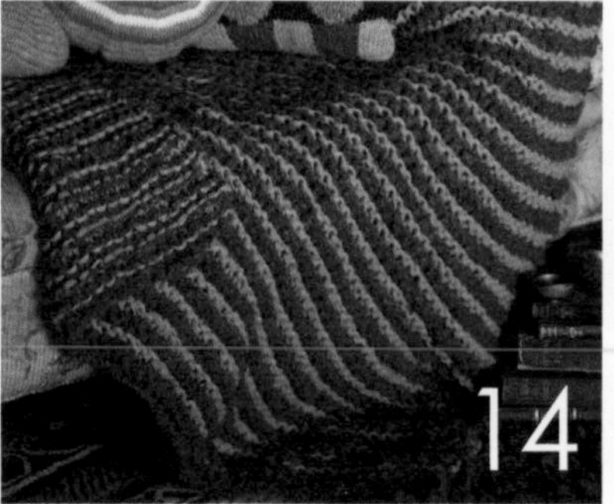

garter stitch rug or throw
pattern page 41

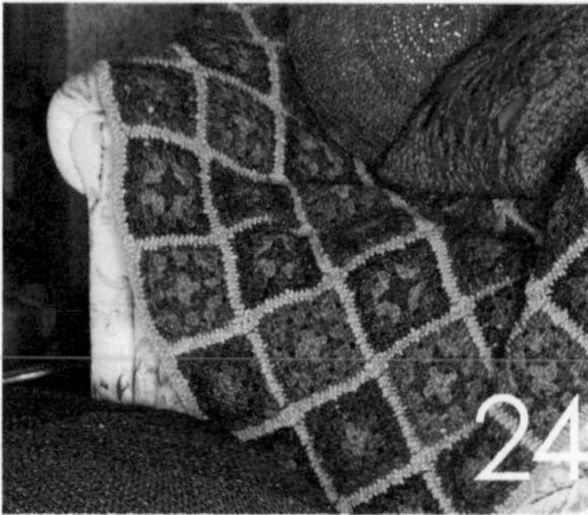

granny squares throw
pattern page 42

crochet squares cushion
pattern page 43

graphics squares cushion
pattern page 44

lattice spot cushion
pattern page 45

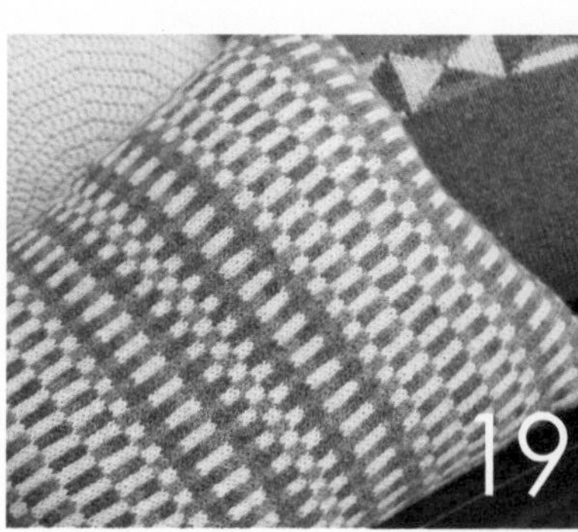

mini graphics cushion
pattern page 46

plaited place mat
pattern page 47

textured rug
pattern page 48

tweed throw
pattern page 49

two tone stripe cushion
pattern page 51